PARAKEETS

by Elaine Radford

Photography by: Dr. Herbert R. Axelrod, Isabelle Francais, Michael Gilroy, H. Lacey, Horst Mayer, Susan C. Miller, Robert Pearcy, Marvin Roberts, Vincent Serbin, Louise B. Van der Meid, Norma Veich and Wayne Wallace.

yearBOOK

Beautiful, intelligent, affectionate, and easy to care for, Budgerigars (Parakeets as known in the U.S.) have steadily grown in popularity as pets. As the smallest member of the parrot family, Parakeets are appealing because they allow people to have a little piece of the hookbill fancy without incurring the expense of the larger parrot-like birds. Parakeets do well in most situations. Whether you live alone or have a big family, Parakeets learn to rearrange their sleeping and play times to accommodate you. They thrive on affection and return it tenfold. Adding to their appeal is the fact that Parakeets easily learn to whistle little tunes and even can mimic a few words. In the following pages author Elaine Radford effectively educates the reader on all aspects of the Parakeet-keeping hobby. Those who are thinking about acquiring one of these delightful birds or simply are looking for further information will surely benefit from this publication.

What are YearBOOKs?

Because keeping parakeets as a hobby is growing at a rapid pace, information on their selection, care and breeding is vitally needed in the marketplace. Books, the usual way information of this sort is transmitted, can be too slow. Sometimes by the time a book is written and published, the material contained therein is a year or two old...and no new material has been added during that time. Only a book in a magazine form can bring breaking stories and current information. A magazine is streamlined in production, so we have adopted certain magazine publishing techniques in the creation of this yearBOOK. Magazines also can be much cheaper than books because they are supported by advertising. To combine these assets into a great publication, we issued this yearBOOK in both magazine and book format at different prices.

yearBOOKS,INC.
Dr. Herbert R. Axelrod,
Founder & Chairman

Neal Pronek
Chief Editor
Bill Starika
Editor

yearBOOKS are all photo composed, color separated and designed on Scitex equipment in Neptune, N.J. with the following staff:

COMPUTER ART
Michael L. Secord
Supervisor
Sherise Buhagiar
Patti Escabi
Cynthia Fleureton
Sandra Taylor Gale
Pat Marotta
Joanne Muzyka
Robert Onyrscuk
Tom Roberts

Advertising Sales
George Campbell
Chief
Amy Manning
Coordinator

©yearBOOKS,Inc.
1 TFH Plaza
Neptune, N.J.07753
Completely manufactured in Neptune, N.J. • USA

Contents

There's no need for humans to create the dream pet of the twenty-first century...it is known as the Budgerigar, "Budgie" for short.

INTRODUCING THE BUDGERIGAR

In the future scientists may be able to design pets to order. They'll probably start by making up a list of qualities the dream pet should possess: beauty, intelligence, gentleness, hardiness, love for its owner, and the ability to thrive in small apartments on low-cost diets. It would also be nice if the pet were inexpensive and came in a range of decorator colors. And wouldn't it be terrific if it could whistle a pretty

The Budgerigar possesses a long list of good qualities. It is beautiful, intelligent, gentle, hardy, affectionate...not to mention inexpensive to keep.

tune or even talk?

There's no need for humans to create the dream pet of the twenty-first century. Nature, in the semiarid Australian interior, shaped this friendly, sociable, and hardy pet millenia ago. Scientists named it *Melopsittacus undulatus*. We call it the Budgerigar, "Budgie" for short.

We may also call it one of several other names, although we're usually creating some confusion in the process. Most people in the United States habitually refer to the Budgerigar as the "parakeet," an imprecise name because many other species of parrots are also called parakeets. At least many of these other parakeets resemble the Budgerigar in making good pets and fine talkers, and no real harm is done if the readers of certain historical novels get the mistaken impression that Alexander the Great was charmed by a snub-beaked Budgie! A more dangerous nickname for the Budgie was "lovebird." This title was encouraged in the 1920s when a Japanese prince bought a then rare blue pair for his fiancée, sparking a Japanese fashion for giving Budgies as a token of love. Since the true lovebird has a very different personality from the Budgerigar, a confused pet buyer could be in for a real disappointment; fortunately, this mistaken usage has just about vanished. Other names that you may or may not encounter include shell parakeet, warbling parakeet, or canary parrot.

Incidentally, the Budgie's full common name comes from the one quality not important in the dream pet—its taste! The word "Budgerigar" derives from an Australian Aboriginal term that means "good food."

ITS LIFE IN THE WILD

The wild Budgie is a social bird, traveling in flocks containing up to one hundred birds. These flocks often gather into clouds of hundreds of thousands or even millions of individuals. Since the rainfall in the Australian interior is irregular and unpredictable, Budgies are strong fliers that follow food and water rather than migrating according to some fixed pattern. When they chance upon a good supply of both, they waste no time going to nest to produce as many young as they possibly can before the opportunity passes. Tough and adaptable, they triumph over their harsh environment, replacing their population quickly even after such disasters as the drought of 1932, and the widespread brush fires of 1974, both of which took the lives of millions of Budgerigars.

It's this challenging environment that makes the Budgie the pet it is. Adapted to foraging in arid and semiarid grasslands rather than lush tropical rainforests, it survives and even reproduces on simple seed diets that would kill many other parrot species. Born to travel and breed in constant contact with its own kind, it is gentle and easy-going, qualities that make it an ideal companion for small children as well as a cheerful and cooperative flock member. Forced to actively hunt for the best breeding conditions rather than passively follow a fixed migration route, it's alert, intelligent, and eager to communicate—qualities that make for a wonderful and trainable pet.

To test the Budgerigar's hardiness scientists denied water to ten laboratory specimens. At 80°F and 30% humidity, the birds did well and lost little weight, even after 38 days without drinking. At lower temperatures, some individuals survived for over 4 months without water. It's worth noting that the Australian environment produced two other popular, hardy pet birds, the Zebra Finch and the Cockatiel.

The wild Budgie is similar to the Normal Light Green bird seen in captivity, although the wild bird tends to be quite a bit smaller. With its golden head and striped back, it resembles a sun-dappled leaf when it sits quietly on its favorite perch in a eucalyptus tree. An entire flock of ten to one hundred birds sharing the same tree, are amazingly hard to spot. Their ability to sit

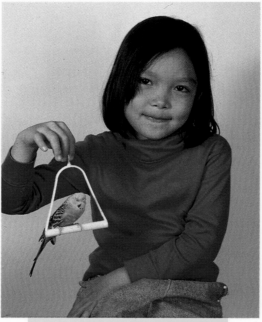

The Budgerigar is alert, intelligent, and eager to communicate— qualities that make for a wonderful and trainable pet.

incredibly still (a technique that helps their bodies conserve water) also aids their disguise as a tree full of bright flowers and young leaves. The few differently colored wild Budgies usually don't survive because they're so easily picked out by predators.

The eucalyptus provides nesting holes as well as protective coloration, and whenever possible, the whole flock will try to nest in one tree, even if some pairs must make their homes in the tangle of roots on the ground. If food and water permit, the race against time to produce young begins as if at the sound of a shot. Any pairs not yet in breeding condition are soon stimulated by the sight of the busy pairs around them. The cock and hen quickly form an efficient partnership that yields healthy young in a short time. The hen incubates the eggs without interruption, the male bringing food to the female so that she doesn't have to leave the nest. When the young are first hatched, the cock continues to feed his hen, while she in turn gives the hatchlings predigested food regurgitated from her crop. When the chicks are a little larger, she leaves the nesthole to help her mate find food for the demanding babies. Still later, if conditions permit, she'll start laying the next clutch while the male weans the fledglings. The quick, efficient breeding habits of the Budgerigar are another reason, of course, that these lively birds have become affordable common pets.

VARIETIES

Today, you can walk into the smallest pet store and examine Budgies in a range of colors. Once human

Today, we can walk into the smallest pet store and examine Budgies in a wide range of colors.

project by buying the dark grays that would be produced along the way. It may not be possible to develop a red Budgie, since it's a primary color that can't be created by mixing the pigments already present in the Budgie's genes. But you never know. Blue is also a primary color, and it's easily produced in these birds, thanks to an optical quirk that couldn't have been predicted ahead of time. Perhaps one day a lucky breeder will find that some unexpected combination of birds has produced the long-awaited red Budgie. Some eager breeders have tried to help the process along by mating Budgies with some of the small grass parakeets that do possess a red pigment, but so far all of these hybrids have proved sterile.

Don't be fooled by sellers offering Budgies that have been fed color food or even dyed to produce a temporarily pink or reddish bird. The breeder who succeeds in producing the red Budgie won't have to look for buyers! In 1927, a pair of the new blue Budgies went for as much as $1,000. Taking into account the much greater difficulty in encountering and developing a red Budgie, not to mention the effects of the intervening years of high inflation, a red Budgie breeder could certainly command a much, much higher price.

But you needn't spend a king's ransom to get a perfect pet in a beautiful color. Lovely blue, white, yellow, and green Budgies are all available at roughly the same price. Since color and pattern have no effect on the Budgie's personality, you can get the prettiest bird in the shop without sacrificing a thing in terms of friendliness, gentleness, or intelligence. No need to worry about that beautiful Sky Blue Budgie turning out to have a fussy, fancy personality; the pretty Budgie is just as sweet as a plain one. Take your time, have fun looking them over, and feel free to go for the one you want.

You needn't spend a king's ransom to get a perfect pet in a beautiful color. Lovely blue, white, yellow, and green budgies are all available at roughly the same price.

CHOOSING YOUR BUDGERIGAR

Almost every home or lifestyle has room for Budgies, but not everyone has room for one Budgie. Contradictory? Not at all. Remember, the Budgerigar is an extremely social bird. It may live longer without water than without companionship! In the early days of Budgie keeping, many people believed that these birds would die if kept from their mates. They were only partially correct. Sex and courtship are hard work for these conscientious birds, and unmated Budgies actually have a longer life expectancy than good breeders. It's lack of love and companionship that's fatal. If you don't have the time to spend with your Budgie virtually every day, it will become depressed and susceptible to disease, sometimes even mutilating itself by tearing out its own feathers. If you travel or party frequently, or spend long hours at the office, you shouldn't try to keep a single pet Budgie. Get two and let these cheerful little socialites entertain each other.

Conversely, if you are a parent selecting a child's pet, or an invalid or a home office worker who requires a companion to share long hours each day, you should opt for a single Budgie. Don't get a pair, hoping to train both birds at once; they'll be too involved with playing with one another to get interested in their lessons.

CHOOSING A HEALTHY BUDGIE

No matter what the time of year, you won't have much trouble finding Budgies for sale. Bred indoors, with abundant food and water,

Your local pet shop will have a wide selection of books by T.F.H. for you to read up on the care and maintenance of Budgies.

they can and do breed in any season. Many excellent birds are available in spring, since breeders of exhibition Budgies start their pairs in late winter or early spring in order to allow plenty of time to prepare for the autumn shows. After

selecting the young nearest the "ideal," these breeders sell the others to stores or individuals. These culls may not be as beefy or come in as many rare colors as the top show quality birds, but they can make wonderfully entertaining and attractive pets. Christmastime also finds plenty of lovable Budgies for sale, especially inexpensive specimens bred in aviaries specifically for the pet trade.

Whether you buy your Budgie from a shop, an aviary, or the back room of somebody's home, you need to look for evidence of health and care. Cleanliness is essential. Although any place where many birds are bred may become somewhat dusty, the dust situation shouldn't be raging so far out of control that you can't breathe without violent sneezing. Certainly, there shouldn't be any offensive odors! Budgies are naturally tidy individuals. As seed-eaters, they produce compact, odorless feces that fall neatly to the bottom of the cage; as strong fliers, they spend a great deal of time keeping their feathers clean and ready for use. If their cages and plumage are filthy, you can bet that they've either come down with an illness or are just about to.

The primary hallmark of a good seller is concern. That means concern for the birds, who won't be so crowded together that they've started fighting and yanking out one is it? Only Mother Nature knows for sure.

Don't worry. Unless you're a serious breeder, in which case you will begin to develop the sensitive eye necessary to sex Budgies correctly most of the time, you needn't be concerned. A pair of Budgies will enjoy playing with each other just as much if they turn out to be members of the same sex. They won't be able to breed, of course, but most single pairs don't breed in any case. Because they're colony breeders, they rarely get the urge to reproduce unless they see other Budgies around them doing the same thing. If you do want to try breeding, start with two or three pairs containing birds of known sex.

WELCOMING THE NEW BUDGIE

The first few days in its new home are important to the Budgie. Don't make it spend this crucial period of orientation in a cardboard box or an undersized travel cage! The permanent cage should be ready and waiting for the new pet in a quiet, draft-free location. A low-key corner of a den or living room is great because it allows the bird to observe the comings and goings of family members without feeling under observation itself. The kitchen, on the other hand, must be off-limits because of cooking odors, aerosol sprays, and other respiratory irritants that can overwhelm a small bird's system. Be especially careful to keep the Budgie away from freshly painted rooms or natural gas.

If the new pet isn't yet tame, it will be understandably cautious about its new environment. Don't rush it. Let it spend the first few days looking around and getting acquainted with the surroundings. In addition to its usual seed cup and water bowl, scatter some small seed or a strand of millet spray along the floor in case the nervous Budgie reverts to its ground-feeding instincts. Keep an eye on the Budgie, but don't pester it with attention for the moment. Give it time to relax enough to eat and drink before you consider taming.

Budgies can sit very still, especially if they don't want to be noticed, so don't be alarmed if your new pet is sitting there like a little stone. It will come around. You just need to give it a chance to figure out that no one is going to hurt it. The young Budgie will probably start eating sooner if you start it on the same food it was fed by the seller. Any changes in diet should be reserved for a less stressful period. Don't expect to see the Budgie eat; it probably won't crack seed in front of you until it trusts you better. In the unusual event that you don't find empty seed husks on the bottom of the cage or within its bowl after 24 hours, you may then conclude that the bird isn't eating and contact the seller for help.

Most likely, your Budgie will be eating by the next day, resigned to its new home if not yet delighted with it. At this point, you'll be ready to tame and train your new pet, helping it become a member of the family as well as a beloved avian companion.

> **Do not make your new Budgie spend its first few days in its new home in a cardboard box or an undersized travel cage! The permanent cage should be ready and waiting for the new pet in a quiet, draft-free location.**

YOUR BUDGERIGAR'S HOME

If you've never kept a pet bird before, you may have the idea that a tame Budgie doesn't really need a cage. Some people even feel that they're doing their bird a kindness by letting it have the freedom of the house at all hours of the day and night. Wrong! Like most pet birds, the Budgie likes having a place of its own where it can retreat to eat and drink, sleep unmolested, or just rest up until it's ready for the next round of family play. Unless its cage is cruelly confining or it's trapped there for days on end without attention, the Budgie considers the cage its home.

Although you certainly should allow your Budgie plenty of free flight time when you're home to supervise, you also need a cage to keep the Budgie safe while you're out of the house. Otherwise, your curious winged pet could easily stumble onto some fatal mischief. If you have children, you know how difficult it is to childproof the average home against a crawling, relatively weak toddler. Multiply the difficulties involved when it's a sturdy little hookbill who can fly up to seek out trouble if it can't find any on the ground, and you start to get an idea of the magnitude of the problem. Furthermore, the tiny Budgie can poison itself on a bit of houseplant or a dab of spilled chemical that the much larger child wouldn't

even notice. Even if you're a scrupulous housekeeper, you can't hope to see your Budgie live out a normal lifespan if you allow it to roam free in your absence.

Therefore, you need a cage. But what kind of cage? Don't expect it to live in one of those small traveling cages sometimes included in package deals. Unless someone is with the bird all day so that it only has to return to the cage to eat and sleep, that tiny area simply isn't enough for an active,

with a pet parrot all day? When you can't be with your Budgie, it will be in its cage and it will both want and need room enough to turn around without crimping its tail!

> **Both you and your Budgie will prefer a cage that's easy to clean. A removable tray bottom is essential to easy removal of the wastes that fall to the bottom of the cage.**

lively bird. Please be realistic before nodding your head and saying, "Yeah, yeah, I'm home all the time. He can sleep in the traveler." You may be home, but will your shoulder really be available at all hours to serve as the Budgie's playpen? Are there really never days when you feel too harassed or busy or just plain sick to keep up

Because the cage will be a play area as well as a bedroom, I strongly advise that you choose one at least 2 feet in length for a single pet Budgie. A pair also needs a minimum of $2' \times 1\frac{1}{2}' \times 1\frac{1}{2}'$ Don't scrimp. Yes, the pet shop probably did keep several Budgies in the same amount of an area space because these birds are

EMERGENCY AND VACATION DIET

When you're on vacation or for some other reason must have a caretaker feed your Budgies, you needn't fret about simplifying the diet back to the old standby of basic seed and water for a week or two as long as the birds aren't breeding. It's prolonged deprivation that hurts the hardy Budgie, not a brief vacation from the perfect diet. After an ignorant friend cheerily informed me that he hadn't had to feed my parrot all week (fortunately, this bird was substantially larger than a Budgie and lived through the experience), I insisted that pet sitters *completely* empty seed dishes and fill them with fresh seed every day. Otherwise, memories of a beautiful vacation could be ruined by a sitter starving a Budgie to death because its seed dish is "filled" with empty husks.

A tame, confident pet will be much bolder about sampling a wide variety of healthy treats. It may become quite adept at snatching food from *your* plate!

PIGS AND PICKY EATERS

Most Budgies don't care for changes in their diet, so it's best to establish a healthy routine early. You have no control over what the bird ate before it came home with you, so make any necessary changes slowly. As the youngster grows tame it will be more willing to accept new foods. A tame, confident pet will be much bolder about sampling a wide variety of healthy treats. It may become quite adept at snatching food from *your* plate!

If you eat nutritiously, you need not be overly concerned about banning the Budgie from the dinner table. Fresh and lightly cooked foods such as salads, vegetables, and fruits can be offered without fear. Small amounts of whole grain breads and brown grains are also fine, as is a smidgen of chicken or other lean meat. Avoid offering cakes, pies, cookies, candies, or other sweets. Sugar is a wonderful perverter of taste buds in birds as well as humans, and you may never enjoy another peaceful snack again once you introduce it to your Budgie. One author wrote that he had to ban ice cream from his home for the duration of his pet Budgie's lifetime, thanks to its pitiful crying when it caught sight of the forbidden food!

An overindulged Budgie may quickly become overweight. In that case, restrict table foods to vegetables and fruits without dollops of dressing, butter, or margarine. Let it concentrate on food that's work (or play) to eat, such as millet spray or a fruit tree twig. Never force a Budgie to fast, no matter how fat! If it must lose weight quickly for health reasons, work out a safe diet with your vet. I personally feel it's better to let the bird lose weight slowly, by encouraging it to play and exercise more often while eating a diet free of high calorie treats.

Adult birds can be picky eaters if they didn't learn good habits early. If you bought them for a breeding project, you're especially anxious to feed them nutritiously, yet they may be especially anxious to maintain the status quo. Tempt them by sprinkling their softfood with a bit of favorite seed, and try boiled egg as a source of vitamin and proteins. Don't give up too soon. You may have to throw out uneaten cups of good food for days or weeks until the birds are used to its presence and ready to sample. Be patient, and the Budgies should come around. It's best not to provide the nest box until they are eating the protein foods, otherwise they won't be in condition for producing topnotch young. There's no hurry. As I said at the beginning, feeding the Budgie is really quite easy, so why not do it right?

CHOOSING YOUR BUDGERIGAR

Almost every home or lifestyle has room for Budgies, but not everyone has room for one Budgie. Contradictory? Not at all. Remember, the Budgerigar is an extremely social bird. It may live longer without water than without companionship! In the early days of Budgie keeping, many people believed that these birds would die if kept from their mates. They were only partially correct. Sex and courtship are hard work for these conscientious birds, and unmated Budgies actually have a longer life expectancy than good breeders. It's lack of love and companionship that's fatal. If you don't have the time to spend with your Budgie virtually every day, it will become depressed and susceptible to disease, sometimes even mutilating itself by tearing out its own feathers. If you travel or party frequently, or spend long hours at the office, you shouldn't try to keep a single pet Budgie. Get two and let these cheerful little socialites entertain each other.

Conversely, if you are a parent selecting a child's pet, or an invalid or a home office worker who requires a companion to share long hours each day, you should opt for a single Budgie. Don't get a pair, hoping to train both birds at once; they'll be too involved with playing with one another to get interested in their lessons.

CHOOSING A HEALTHY BUDGIE

No matter what the time of year, you won't have much trouble finding Budgies for sale. Bred indoors, with abundant food and water,

Your local pet shop will have a wide selection of books by T.F.H. for you to read up on the care and maintenance of Budgies.

they can and do breed in any season. Many excellent birds are available in spring, since breeders of exhibition Budgies start their pairs in late winter or early spring in order to allow plenty of time to prepare for the autumn shows. After

selecting the young nearest the "ideal," these breeders sell the others to stores or individuals. These culls may not be as beefy or come in as many rare colors as the top show quality birds, but they can make wonderfully entertaining and attractive pets. Christmastime also finds plenty of lovable Budgies for sale, especially inexpensive specimens bred in aviaries specifically for the pet trade.

Whether you buy your Budgie from a shop, an aviary, or the back room of somebody's home, you need to look for evidence of health and care. Cleanliness is essential. Although any place where many birds are bred may become somewhat dusty, the dust situation shouldn't be raging so far out of control that you can't breathe without violent sneezing. Certainly, there shouldn't be any offensive odors! Budgies are naturally tidy individuals. As seed-eaters, they produce compact, odorless feces that fall neatly to the bottom of the cage; as strong fliers, they spend a great deal of time keeping their feathers clean and ready for use. If their cages and plumage are filthy, you can bet that they've either come down with an illness or are just about to.

The primary hallmark of a good seller is concern. That means concern for the birds, who won't be so crowded together that they've started fighting and yanking out one another's feathers, as well as concern for you. A concerned seller will ask if you have a proper cage—an individual breeder might not have them for sale anyway—but to make sure the Budgie will have a safe home. The seller should also be willing to answer any questions you may have about bird care in general or the proposed pet in particular.

Before you buy, examine the Budgie as closely as possible to confirm that it's in good health. You may feel sorry for a saggy, moth-eaten bird, but you shouldn't take it into your home. Besides the obvious chance of losing the animal and infecting any other birds you may own, you're imposing an additional stress at a time when the Budgie isn't fit enough to cope. It must remain the seller's responsibility to cure a sick bird before trying to market it. Yes, it's quite possible that the only thing wrong with the bird is that it's being bullied because it's at the bottom of the pecking order in an overcrowded cage. But how can you know for sure that this stress hasn't already weakened the bird enough to let in some serious infection? The best way you can help such animals is by taking your money to another seller, so that stores and breeders will have an economic incentive to stop crowding birds.

Apart from obvious feather damage, discharge from the eyes, nose, and vent are all serious symptoms, as are feces caked thickly around the vent. A deformed beak or

weak, twisted legs can indicate an inherited defect or the incurable legacy of an early nutritional problem. Although the bird may sit very still, as if hoping to avoid drawing your attention, it should certainly be alert and responsive when you come near. If all else checks out, ask the seller to catch the Budgie for your inspection. Probe under its feathers gently. If the keelbone (located in the chest) feels like the blade of a knife, the bird is too underweight to endure the stress of relocation. If you feel strange bumps or swelling, the bird may be one of the many Budgerigars plagued by

> **Before you buy, examine the Budgie as closely as possible to confirm that it's in good health.**

harmful tumors and must be rejected.

Some Budgies have an odd ring of feathers on their heads. That isn't a problem, it's a crest! Three kinds of crests exist: the tufted, which consists of just a few raised feathers on top of the head, the half-crested, which has a small neat cap, and the full-crested, which seems to have an early Beatles' style hairdo. Since they're hard to breed reliably and may have health problems, crested Budgies are usually not offered to beginners. If you do get a crested Budgie, remember never to pair it with another crested, since the offspring of such unions has a very low survival rate.

CHOOSING THE BEST PET

If you want a true feathered companion, a bird that will play with you, spend

hours riding around the house on your shoulder, and even learn to do tricks and talk, choose a Budgie that's young and adaptable. It isn't necessary to buy a handfed baby (although that's certainly nice if one is available) since Budgies are easily trained up to the age of 3 months. The younger, the better, of course, as long as the babies are weaned and able to feed themselves, a process that should be finished by 6 weeks.

It's easy to make sure that a Budgie is young enough to make a good pet for a beginner. Babies' heads and necks are covered with a network of shell-like stripes that start to disappear at 10 or 12 weeks. Babies also look big-eyed because the iris (ring of color surrounding the pupil) is black; as they mature, this ring lightens noticeably. Very young babies have darker

If you want a true feathered companion, a bird that will play with you, spend hours riding around the house on your shoulder, and even learn to do tricks and talk, choose a Budgie that's young and adaptable.

beaks; if a prospective pet is feeding itself, yet still has some black on the beak, it's at the perfect age for training as a companion.

CHOOSING A PAIR

If you have little time to spend training your birds, but would like some color and life in your home, you will have to pick two healthy Budgies. Age isn't as crucial since you won't be training them as pets, but it does reduce stress on the birds if they are moved

into their new home while young, especially if they have come from an aviary where they weren't used to living in close contact with admiring humans every day. Feel free to mix and match colors as you please; Budgies have no prejudices!

Are you wondering how to get a "true" pair—one boy, one girl? Adult budgies are relatively easy to sex, at least when you compare them to some species of parrots that look so much alike it's a mystery how they themselves can tell. The general rule involves checking the cere, the flesh around the nostrils. In most males, at least while in breeding condition, the cere is bright blue, while most females have brown ceres. Some Budgies, however, particularly among the lighter color forms, may have ceres that look blue in one light, pinkish tan in another. What is it? Only Mother Nature knows for sure.

Don't worry. Unless you're a serious breeder, in which case you will begin to develop the sensitive eye necessary to sex Budgies correctly most of the time, you needn't be concerned. A pair of Budgies will enjoy playing with each other just as much if they turn out to be members of the same sex. They won't be able to breed, of course, but most single pairs don't breed in any case. Because they're colony breeders, they rarely get the urge to reproduce unless they see other Budgies around them doing the same thing. If you do want to try breeding, start with two or three pairs containing birds of known sex.

WELCOMING THE NEW BUDGIE

The first few days in its new home are important to the Budgie. Don't make it spend this crucial period of orientation in a cardboard box or an undersized travel cage! The permanent cage should be ready and waiting for the new pet in a quiet, draft-free location. A low-key corner of a den or living room is great because it allows the bird to observe the comings and goings of family members without feeling under observation itself. The kitchen, on the other hand, must be off-limits because of cooking odors, aerosol sprays, and other respiratory irritants that can overwhelm a small bird's system. Be especially careful to keep the Budgie away from freshly painted rooms or natural gas.

If the new pet isn't yet tame, it will be understandably cautious about its new environment. Don't rush it. Let it spend the first few days looking around and getting acquainted with the surroundings. In addition to its usual seed cup and water bowl, scatter some small seed or a strand of millet spray along the floor in case the nervous Budgie reverts to its ground-feeding instincts. Keep an eye on the Budgie, but don't pester it with attention for the moment. Give it time to relax enough to eat and drink before you consider taming.

Budgies can sit very still, especially if they don't want to be noticed, so don't be alarmed if your new pet is sitting there like a little stone. It will come around. You just need to give it a chance to figure out that no one is going to hurt it. The young Budgie will probably start eating sooner if you start it on the same food it was fed by the seller. Any changes in diet should be reserved for a

less stressful period. Don't expect to see the Budgie eat; it probably won't crack seed in front of you until it trusts you better. In the unusual event that you don't find empty seed husks on the bottom of the cage or within its bowl after 24 hours, you may then conclude that the bird isn't eating and contact the seller for help.

Most likely, your Budgie will be eating by the next day, resigned to its new home if not yet delighted with it. At this point, you'll be ready to tame and train your new pet, helping it become a member of the family as well as a beloved avian companion.

Do not make your new Budgie spend its first few days in its new home in a cardboard box or an undersized travel cage! The permanent cage should be ready and waiting for the new pet in a quiet, draft-free location.

An over indulged Budgie may quickly become overweight. In that case, restrict table foods to vegetables and fruits without dollops of dressing, butter, or margarine.

TAMING AND TRAINING

The younger the Budgie, the more success you'll have with training. A newly weaned youngster is ideal, while an adult can be close to untamable. Assuming you chose a youngster for your pet, however, you'll find the taming process easy and enjoyable even if you've never tamed a parrot before.

Whether or not you intend to keep the Budgie's wings clipped after it's tame, you should probably start by having the seller clip a few of the flight feathers. A Budgie raised by its own parents is naturally very shy of large humans, and you could traumatize it badly if you must chase it around the training room with a net! Also, it's safer if the bird gets to know the layout of the home before it's capable of an all-out flight into a win-

Your new pet Budgerigar will have to be taught that it is safe to sit on your bare hand.

dow or wall. Do ask the seller to perform this chore since you don't want your pet to form its first impressions of you while you're holding it down to trim its feathers.

It's possible to hand-tame a young Budgie in fifteen minutes, although most people prefer to spread the

A baby Budgie is unlikely to bite you, especially if you take the gradual approach, and in any case, it will certainly not inflict any real damage.

process out over a period of days. If for some reason you're taming an adult or a previously abused bird, you *must* proceed slowly, rebuilding the Budgie's trust over a period of weeks or even months. Intensive taming helps you to take advantage of the Budgie's peak learning period between five and ten

The Budgie learns most quickly when it has nothing to distract it from the attentions of its trainer.

weeks of age, but since this method is quite stressful, it should be reserved for healthy, well-fed specimens no more than nine or ten weeks old.

Either a simple hand-held perch or a T-shaped perch called a T-stick is advisable to help taming go more smoothly. I don't suggest wearing gloves unless you are extremely nervous or sensitive to pain. The baby Budgie is unlikely to bite you, especially if you take the gradual approach, and in any case, it will certainly not inflict any real damage. By using the gloves, you have only added another step to the taming, since the bird will have to be taught later that it's safe to sit on your bare hand.

INTENSIVE TAMING

Caution: This method should only be used for healthy, young Budgies who are eating well in their new home!

Although it's cracking seed, your new Budgie is probably most reluctant to leave its cage.

Open the cage. The Budgie is unlikely to leap for its freedom, as you may suppose; it usually prefers to cower behind bars. It's up to you to get it out.

It may not seem to do much at all, in fact, except sit very still and hope it's escaping notice. You may wonder if that quivering heap of feathers will really become a pet. Never fear! You should see it begin to gain its confidence this very night.

Clear the room containing the cage of all fragile knick knacks, spiny houseplants, drinking glasses, or other hazards. Cover any aquariums and windows. Close all doors, locking any that lead directly outside. Any pets must be moved to another room, and other birds should be out of earshot as well as out of sight. Turn off the TV and the stereo. The Budgie learns most quickly when it has nothing to distract it from the attentions of its

trainer. Only one person should handle the job of training, to avoid confusing the Budgie. It can be introduced to the rest of the family once it has had a chance to decide that humans are OK.

Now you may open the cage. The Budgie is unlikely to leap for its freedom, as you may suppose; it usually prefers to cower behind bars. It's up to you to get it out. Although you wouldn't put your hand in the cage of a large parrot, who even if tame would react with outrage to this invasion of its territory, it's perfectly safe to put your hand into your Budgie's cage. Slowly! Make

When you hold your finger at chest height—you may have to nudge the Budgie gently—it will eventually be unable to resist the temptation to step aboard.

your movements almost imperceptible, and talk in a low, soothing voice the whole time. If you can, approach the bird from its side so that it can see you clearly out of one eye. It will feel less threatened if you approach quietly, head-on

towards its blind spot, like a predator preparing to pounce!

The untame Budgie may flutter toward you as if to bite (but rarely doing more than feinting), or huddle away from you, crying with fear. Stop moving your hand forward when it panics, but don't retreat. Otherwise, it will think it can scare you off and repeat these behaviors whenever you attempt training. When it calms somewhat, slowly move your hand forward once more. Your aim is to sidle up to the Budgie's chest to take advantage of the bird's natural desire to step up. When you hold your finger at chest height—you may have to nudge the Budgie gently—it will eventually be unable to resist the temptation to step aboard. At that point, you may start to very slowly remove your hand from the cage. Be patient. The Budgie may hop off and on several times before you convince it to ride out into the open air. Notice the time. If more than fifteen or twenty minutes have

A bird that walks on you with confidence if not enthusiasm is technically tame, but it should be trained to be held in the hand.

One of the most valuable tricks you can teach your Budgie is to "come" on command. Once it's flying freely to your shoulder, you should have little difficulty with this trick.

tricks by teaching them to associate certain actions with a food reward, can make successful performing artists of Budgies and other birds that are not even technically tame. However, at home trick training is usually based on affection. The Budgie shows off to win a beloved human's admiration, with a food treat being only a secondary enticement for a good performance. Therefore, a tame Budgie who loves its owner will learn tricks much faster than an untame bird.

One of the most valuable tricks you can teach your Budgie is to "come" on command. Once it's flying freely to your shoulder, you should have little difficulty with this trick. Place the Budgie on top of its playpen or cage, and tell it to "come." Have a food treat ready for when it obeys. Of course, the first few times it may fly to you simply because it wants to, it has no idea it's doing a trick at all. But if you practice faithfully, rewarding the Budgie each time it comes to you on command, it should eventually learn to associate the word with the desired action. A sharp Budgie may even learn to say the word "come" itself, and to be fair, I guess you better obey!

Very patient people have also taught their Budgies to defecate on command in their playpens or cages. It's easier just to wear a lot of old shirts when the Budgie's at large, but a housetrained bird is certainly a nice thing to have. To work this trick, you must think of a word that will never, ever come up in conversation for the command to

defecate. (Actually, "defecate" itself is fine; at least, it isn't something that *my* friends often discuss!) You must also be observant enough to notice the subtle signs that the Budgie is about to defecate, usually a slight squatting just beforehand. At first, content yourself with giving the command every time you see the Budgie doing its business in cage or playpen so that it will begin to associate the word with the act. Later,

A tame bird loves learning tricks because it can use them to amuse itself as well as to get the attention of its owners.

when you're playing with the Budgie and notice that it's about to relieve itself hastily place it atop its cage and give the command. You'll have to be patient and tolerant of accidents for days or weeks, but eventually you should arrive at a point where you can drop the Budgie off at its

cage, give the word, and have it go. Understand, however, that even a well-trained Budgie isn't built to hold it. To prevent accidents, return it to cage or portable playpen every 20 minutes and give it the command.

Let me assure the anxious that accidents are no real problem unless you make a habit of black tie and evening dress at home. Bird droppings come out of washable clothes without any special effort on your part.

No one objects to practical tricks, but some people may have misconceptions about "fun" tricks. It is not cruel to teach your Budgie tricks. In fact, a tame bird loves learning tricks because it can use them to amuse itself as well as to get the attention of its owners. The proof is the many Budgies who will do their tricks when they're playing alone. Actually, it is a kindness to teach tricks because it prevents the bird from becoming bored and listless. In the wild, the Budgie would spend hours each day foraging for food and avoiding predators. In captivity, it needs another use for its clever brain, and what better than tricks which amuse pet and owner alike? Working together to learn tricks forges a deep tie of affection between bird and human. Despite the hundreds of thousands of Budgies in this country, you will have great difficulty purchasing a tame and talking trick bird. Most people simply won't give them up for any price.

The simplest tricks take advantage of the Budgie's

pitched voices seem easier for Budgies to imitate, so if your voice is low, try to pitch it higher for the duration of the lesson. You may feel silly, but only until you impress all your friends with your pet's speaking abilities!

Rhythmic speech catches the Budgie's attention and is more easily imitated than monotonous speech. Always try to choose phrases that lend themselves to enthusiastic, rhythmic inflection. Questions are especially good because they are naturally inflected upward at the end of the sentence. For example, "Got a cracker?" is naturally more tuneful (not to mention more gracious) than "I wanna cracker."

Once they've got the hang of it, Budgies will pick up additional words on their own, although not as fast as they would if you continued teaching them. For that reason, avoid obscenities and profanities around the Budgie. It may seem "cute" the first time you hear your pet repeat an objectionable phrase in all innocence, but it won't seem very funny when it says it in front of your boss, the next-door neighbor's kid, or a gathering of the family clan. It is unfair to remove a bird so eager to entertain and please from family and social life just because you were careless, so do your best to prevent the Budgie from hearing these words.

If you work during the day, you can purchase phonographs or tapes so that the Budgie can hear its lessons while you're away. (In fact, you can even buy videos of an actual parrot talking!) However, be aware that the recorded lessons are a supplement, not a replacement for personal lessons. Always spend some time in the evenings with the Budgie perched on your finger to watch *you* repeat the desired phrase.

WHISTLING AND SINGING

It's easy to teach a Budgie to whistle, although you should wait until it's speaking clearly to begin music lessons. Otherwise, it may concentrate on the whistling, which is more natural to its ears, and completely ignore the less musical words. Don't go too fast. Start with one bar of music, and go on to the next when the Budgie has perfected that one. Remember to always start each melody from the beginning so the Budgie will know that the individual bars form a whole tune.

Some Budgies have learned to sing, but this is very difficult. You must teach a simple tune in a high key, and be prepared to spend many months to teach a single song at the rate of a bar or two at a time. A singing Budgie is a testament to the dedication of its owner.

GETTING THE BUDGIE TO TALK TO COMPANY

Nothing is more infuriating than a talented little talker who clams up when friends come over to admire it, but the Budgie has perfectly logical reasons for its frustrating behavior. As far as it's concerned, it learned to talk to win the attention and admiration of its person. Since it doesn't want the attention of strangers—whose motives, after all, are totally unknown to the bird—it stays quiet. Fortunately, you can make your pet change its mind if you and your friends are patient.

The simplest thing to do is to ignore the bird and entertain your friends. After an hour or so, when the Budgie has seen that they're harmless, it will often decide that it wants to join the fun and calls out an eager, "Hi there!" But to make this technique work, you must prevent your friends from focusing on the bird. If they're all standing around the cage waiting, the Budgie will sense the tension and stay quiet, speaking up only after you've closed the door on your last visitor.

Since Budgies feel chatty when they have the opportunity to interrupt, you can often speed up the proceedings by providing a little background noise. Surprisingly, many chirp right up when the tap water's running or the vacuum cleaner's roaring. Others enjoy speaking to a toy Budgie or their reflection in a mirror, so that if you know guests are coming ahead of time, you can place these items in its cage for encouragement. After several good experiences, you probably won't need these tricks any more. Your Budgie will become a feathered ham, anxious to show off for those big, funny-looking creatures that make such a gratifying fuss when it performs.

It is difficult to teach two Budgies to speak at the same time because their attention is not focused on you.

If you are more interested in breeding for sale or show than home display, you may want to consider a bird room, an entire room converted to the care and breeding of Budgies and their friends.

free color; a pastel green or pale gold might be nice, as are a few graceful ferns or palms painted on the back wall. Don't hang the new door until you've finished the interior, and give it a couple of weeks to air out before placing the birds inside. Safe potted plants can be placed in the aviary, but have enough to rotate them out on a regular basis. Otherwise, your Budgies will chew

them to pieces! You can turn the dirt when you're changing the vegetation. You will notice that the closet aviary is best suited to tame or semi-tame Budgies who will sit on a perch presented to them, since it isn't exactly escape-proof during routine maintenance.

If you are more interested in breeding for sale or show than home display, you may want to consider a bird room, an entire room converted to the care and breeding of Budgies and their friends. Bird rooms can be as simple or as complicated as your individual situation requires. If you are breeding to sell to pet stores or for relaxation, you may prefer to use a few easily maintained flights. You sacrifice control of colors and varieties produced since the Budgies can pick their own partners, but you gain greatly in convenience and saved cleaning time. The serious showperson, however, will certainly prefer setting up racks of individual cages so that he or she can determine which birds mate. Because many separate cages can be difficult to keep clean and well-lighted, I urge you to consult one of the many excellent advanced

books on Budgerigar show breeding before trying to establish this kind of bird room.

AN OUTDOOR AVIARY

Outdoor aviaries have many advantages, free sunshine (which the Budgies use to make vitamin D) and lots of exercise room. An outdoor flight almost always has more space for these active birds to fly and play, and it can make a ho-hum garden into a real pleasure.

However, you must also take into account some big drawbacks before building or contracting for the outdoor aviary. Zoning and problem neighbors often mean that outdoor bird flights are illegal or impossible, or both. Laws meant to restrict backyard poultry keeping can be and often are interpreted to mean that all forms of exterior bird housing are forbidden. Find out what the rules are *before* the concrete's poured; otherwise, you could be ordered to tear down the structure. Even if the law is on your side, be realistic about cranky neighbors. You and I know that Budgies are friendly, cheerful-sounding birds, but a judge only has to hear the word "parrot" to think of a blood-chilling macaw shriek and side with the complaining party. If a neighbor has caused trouble in the past, you can bet he or she will seize the opportunity to get back at you through your birds.

You also have to consider another kind of neighbor, the kind that's only too happy to see the bird building go up. Rats and other rodents will want to steal the bird's food, not caring if they contaminate the grain or frighten a breeding pair. Predators from owls to cats will be interested in dining on the Budgies themselves. Cats and rodents may be trapped or shot, but owls, hawks, and eagles are protected by law. (Besides being threatened, these beneficial birds prevent disease by keeping down the rodent population.) In all cases, your building will need to be modified to keep the Budgies in and the predators out. Because birds present such tempting victims to vandals and thieves, you will also need a security system (including an alarm) sufficient to deter break-ins.

In other words, building an outdoor aviary is a grati-

Always try to pair even pairs of birds together, or all of one sex. Never have too many of one sex otherwise disastrous results could occur.

fying but specialized enterprise. Fortunately, in recent years, publishers have produced several good books on the subject. The better advanced Budgie handbooks also contain detailed plans for outdoor breeding aviaries.

COMPANIONS

A flight complete with vegetation and other bird species can be a pleasant haven or a deadly disaster! I'd like to pass on a few tips that others have learned through trial and error so you won't have to repeat the same mistakes with your Budgies.

The first rule concerns size. Many commercial aviaries do well by allowing one adult bird per square foot of floor area, but this is definitely a minimum. Never try to squeeze in "just one more." Budgies are sociable, but even they need room to breathe! Overcrowded flights invite fighting, nest-robbing, and disease. Please be assured that a few lively, playful birds will look far more impressive than many listless ones packed so close together they can do nothing but quarrel.

Since Budgies are gentle, they

Overcrowded flights invite fighting, nest-robbing, and disease. A few lively, playful birds will look far more impressive than many listless ones packed so closely together.

are safe with smaller birds who won't bother them. Of course, these smaller birds should be bold enough to be able to make their own way in a flightful of larger creatures! Give delicate, rare finches their own cage, and let the Budgie share with some sassy Zebra or Society Finches. Although much larger, Cockatiels can also live pleasantly with Budgies as long as there is enough room. Sometimes a Cockatiel and a Budgie will become very good friends, actually playing together and preening one another despite the difference in size. Most other parrots, however, are not safe companions for Budgies. Even if a large parrot is "sweet," it shouldn't be

When choosing a group of birds for breeding, start with healthy, even tempered adults who are at least one year old.

you to wish to breed. A new Budgie would be viewed as a rival for your attention, not a potential mate. On the other hand, semitame Budgies who are somewhat used to human handling even if they don't much care for it are great breeders because they are less likely to become upset when their owners open their nest boxes to check on the progress of their eggs and chicks.

PREPARING FOR BREEDING

Although Budgies can breed indoors at any time of the year, certain conditions must be met before they will start. First off, the birds must be in top condition, good eaters who are well fed on a healthy diet. Molting Budgies shouldn't be asked

Because they are extremely social birds, a single pair of Budgies rarely breed.

you settle them down too early, you will have a host of problems such as eggbinding, refusal to incubate eggs, and abandonment of chicks. Like humans, Budgies should be mentally as well as physically adult before they try to bring youngsters into the world.

Don't try to mate a tame, talking Budgie. Many people think that their pets want mates because they are wooing their owners with typical avian courting behaviors such as offering regurgitated food and mating with a human hand. Actually, these are the very birds you *shouldn't* try to mate because they are too emotionally involved with

A Budgie must be in top condition, a good eater and fed on a healthy diet before it will start to breed.

to breed because they need all their protein for replacing their feathers. Wait until the molt is over before encouraging them to breed.

Because they are extremely social birds, a single pair of Budgies rarely breed. Even two or three pairs can take their time about settling down. In general, at least 12 to 18 adult Budgies should be present to stimulate breeding. Fortunately for people who want some control over the color and shape of their offspring, that doesn't mean all 18 birds have to be in the same flight! Each pair can do perfectly well in individual cages as long as they can hear and see other Budgies around them. A beginner shouldn't be too horrified by the prospect of starting out with so many birds. The fact that several pairs have synchronized their nesting can make your work a lot easier since you can foster eggs and young chicks of nonfeeding or nervous parents to working nests where they'll be better cared for.

Any rodent or predator problem must be brought under control before setting up for breeding. Budgies aren't interested in raising catfood, so the presence of threatening mammals may prevent them from nesting.

Finally, Budgies must have a nest box. Since they breed in tree cavities in the wild, they have no real nest-building skills, although the female does some chewing to modify the interior to her liking. Fortunately, since they're used to nesting in "found" objects, they settle down nicely in artificial nest boxes. You can buy Budgie nest boxes at pet stores, or you can build your own. A simple plywood box some 10" tall by 6" wide and 6" long, with a 2" diameter hole near the top, works fine. Have a short perch underneath the opening to give feeding birds a place to stand, and chisel a concavity into the floor to prevent the eggs from rolling around. Nest boxes should always be hung high in the cage or flight; otherwise, the Budgies may not accept them.

If your Budgies are al-

ready paired in breeding cages or flying free in a breeding flight, don't give them nest boxes until the other breeding conditions are met. These eager-to-please birds could exhaust themselves, risking infection and death, if they start too early. If your hens and cocks are separated, you may go ahead and put the boxes in with the hens so that they can investigate the nest and maybe indulge in a little chewing to "customize" their homes. Give your hens a couple of weeks to settle into their new cages before adding the cocks. Some people like to introduce the male to the female by placing him in a separate cage where she can look him over for a few days. Divided

Since Budgies breed in tree cavities in the wild, they have no real nest building skills and must therefore have a next box supplied for them.

breeder cages are available for this purpose; when you see the Budgies flirting through the bars of the divider, you can safely remove it to let them mate.

Occasionally, a hen in a cage won't like the cock you have chosen for her and will attack him. Since she can trap and kill a male she doesn't like, remove him at once. In a flight containing many Budgies, the birds can find their own mates as long as you are careful to put in equal numbers of males and

A pair of breeding Budgies' nest box can be checked for eggs or chicks as long as you are careful.

females. Remember to have twice as many nest boxes as pairs to prevent quarreling.

At the same time that you're introducing pairs, you should be gradually increasing the amount of lighting and protein in the diet. Breeding Budgies should have 14 hours of light a day and a constant supply of fresh soft food and greens. The mineral block should be fresh and clean; replace it immediately when it's consumed.

INCUBATING THE EGGS

When the hen is ready to start laying, she'll spend a great deal of time inside the nest box. If your female Budgie has "disappeared" for several days, you can start making daily checks

for eggs. Once laying begins, she will usually lay an egg every other day until she has a complete clutch of four to six eggs.

Sometimes the hen lays extra eggs; clutches of nine and even ten eggs have been recorded. Since it's too exhausting for her to attempt to rear so many chicks at once, you will need to do something about the excess. To find out if you really have a problem, you need to know how many of the eggs are actually fertile. A simple device called a candler is used to test for fertility. More elegant candlers are available from commercial sources, but a home candler is just a box with a bright light bulb inside and a small hole on top. You must wait until ten days after incubation (not laying) to use the candler. Place the egg you want to test in the hole and look through it to the light behind. If you can see reddish "spiders" (blood vessels), you can be sure the egg is fertile. If it's completely clear, it's infertile and should be discarded. It is entirely normal to find an infertile egg or two in a clutch, but you should suspect a nutritional or other problem if *all* of the eggs are infertile.

If you find that you have a hen that has too many fertile eggs, you can transfer some of the eggs into the nests of hens who didn't lay as many. (Mark the transferred eggs with an indelible, odorless pen if you want to keep a record of where they came from!) If you still have leftovers, cull the eggs of inferior birds and keep the eggs of superior specimens. It doesn't matter if a small, unbeautiful hen ends up raising a nest full of a show couple's chicks. She won't know the difference, and you'll be improving the quality of your stock without exhausting the best birds.

Since the hen incubates her eggs day and night, the cock must bring her food. The male Budgie is in most cases an exceptionally solicitous bird, occasionally so concerned with feeding his mate that he neglects to feed himself. Therefore, you

A first hatching, a baby Budgie won't be strong enough to do more than lay around and beg for food from its mother.

need to check on the cock as well as the eggs when you inspect the cage each day. If he loses too much weight, he may start hiding in the nest box for warmth—where he may remain until he starves to death. Watch out. If a male seems cold or suspiciously underweight, remove him to a hospital cage where he will have a chance to recover. If the hen is nearly ready to hatch her eggs, she can probably take care of them herself. If incubation has just begun, however, you should remove the eggs to prevent her from joining her mate in a fit of exhaustion.

WHEN THE PARENTS RAISE THE YOUNG

The first egg will hatch about 18 days after the hen

Only the mother Budgie feeds newly hatched chicks. When they begin to feather out, the cock will also begin feeding.

starts incubation. You may be able to hear the chick peeping from within its cracked shell and decide to help it out, especially since it seems to be taking an ungodly amount of time to break out. Please resist the temptation! If you have never seen an egg hatch anywhere except on a time-elapsed film on TV, you will probably be surprised to learn that it normally takes a very long time for the tiny chick to emerge; in the case of the Budgie, hatching takes around 36 hours. If you "help" it out too soon,

it won't finish absorbing its nutrient-rich yolk and will therefore be too weak to survive for more than a few hours.

Continue checking the nest box daily, but don't hover over the new chicks or you may make the hen too nervous to care for them. You aren't missing much. Baby Budgies are naked, blind, and downright ugly! At first they won't be strong enough to do more than lay around and beg for food from their mother, who will start them out on her own crop milk. As the chicks grow and feather out, the cock will also begin feeding. If all goes well, their little crops will be plump and full at all times, and their bodies will seem to grow almost in front of your eyes.

If Budgie chicks are not given permanent closed bands before ten days of age (preferably at around five days), their feet will already be too large to allow the band to pass over their toes onto their legs. If you are planning on showing your birds, you should obtain in advance specially coded rings from the American Budgerigar Society to prove that you bred them yourself. Banding isn't hard. Gently holding the chick, first slip the ring over the three long toes, then on back over the short toe onto the lower leg. If the last toe doesn't want to pop free, you may help slip it out with a burnt matchstick.

Soon after ringing day, the young Budgies will start feathering out at an amazing rate. By the end of the fourth week or the beginning of the fifth week, fully feath-ered chicks should be beginning to leave the nest, although they will still cry to be fed by their parents. If the hen is impatient to lay another clutch, she may become irritable with these ungainly adolescents and try to peck them or pull their feathers to line her nest. In that case, remove them to a separate cage along with the cock so that he can finish raising them. (You can transfer him back to the hen's cage for an hour or two each afternoon for mating.) Of course if all is going well, you can let both parents wean the chicks.

Once they are cracking seed reliably, which should occur around the end of the sixth week, you should remove them to their own cage for sale, pet taming, or whatever. Remember that their instinct is to feed from the ground, so always have plenty of good seed on the floor until they are eating regularly from the feeder.

Your adult birds will live longer and healthier lives if you do not ask them to raise more than two broods a year. When the second brood is finished, you should remove the nest box to prevent the hen from starting the cycle all over again.

FOSTERING AND HANDREARING CHICKS

You don't have to handfeed Budgies to make them into

If all goes well with your Budgie chicks, their little crops will be plump and full at all times, and their bodies will seem to grow almost in front of your eyes.

good pets since they can still become attached to humans if tamed before the tenth or twelfth week of life. Therefore, don't remove chicks from the nest unless you have to. The parents have more time to fuss over their babies than you do! If a young chick falls from its nest, you should warm it in your hands and return it. (It isn't true that human scent causes birds to reject their broods; most birds have relatively poor senses of smell, anyway.) If you aren't sure which nest it came from, just return it to one with babies about the right size. The parents will feed it along with the rest even if you guessed wrong. If it falls out again, you can assume it's being intentionally

If Budgie chicks are not given permanent closed bands before ten days of age, their feet will already be too large to allow the band to pass over their toes onto their legs.

rejected and should try it in another nest. Sometimes a hen will die or stop feeding her babies. If they are unfeathered, they can be distributed among other nests for feeding by other hens; if feathered, the cock should be able to finish the job himself. The point is that in most cases, the birds can be arranged to do the brooding and feeding so you don't have to.

However, exceptions do occur. If the parents aren't feeding three week or older chicks, you can't foster them to other pairs since at this point, the babies are individual enough to be recognized as intruders. Fortunately, it isn't anywhere near as tedious a job to start handfeeding chicks at this point as it would have been to start at day one. Since they aren't yet fully feathered, you need to make a simple brooder to provide warmth. In the past, many people used a cardboard box with a light bulb close to one side; nowadays, it's becoming popular to place the youngsters in a clean aquarium warmed by a heating pad. Don't bake the chicks; at this stage, they need only be kept around 85°F, not 105. Whatever you use, line the bottom with soft towels or plain paper which can be changed each day. You should also spread a little seed on the bottom of the floor to give them a chance to pick at it and learn what it is.

You can buy a good hand-feeding formula at the pet store, or you can make your own at home. Since you will be hand-feeding only a few birds for a few days, you will come off just as cheaply by using the commercial food. Of course, if you handfeed larger parrots as well, you'll save by making the formula at home, but I needn't give you a recipe since you probably already have a favorite of your own! I will simply remind you that

Occasionally, parent birds stop feeding their young and you may be forced to hand-feed them. You should be familiar with this method in case such a situation arises.

Budgies have a very high protein requirement, so make sure the formula you choose for your Budgies is based on a high protein baby cereal or other high protein ingredient.

At three weeks and older, the Budgies are taking too much thick food to get it through a syringe, so you will

want to feed them with what's called a "parrot spoon," a small plastic spoon with the sides bent to form a funnel for the food. If you can't buy them locally, plastic coffee spoons softened over steam can be shaped into parrot spoons quite easily. The baby food should be heated to about 100°F, hot enough to touch to your lip or wrist but not too cold for the Budgie to digest. Feed the youngsters every two to three hours during the day, sooner if their crops empty early, a bit later if they're still too full to eat. Wipe their faces carefully after each feeding; food left to dry on a baby's face can cause permanent beak abnormalities. Healthy babies can survive throughout the night without feeding, so don't keep yourself up all hours fussing. It's safe to carry the birds to work with you if you cover the brooder with a towel en route to prevent upsetting them. At five weeks, the youngsters shouldn't need the heat source any longer and they should be starting to crack their seed. However, continue to offer formula at intervals throughout the day since it will take some time before they're getting enough nutrition on their own.

BREEDING PROBLEMS AND HOW TO SOLVE THEM

It would be wrong of me to leave you with the impression that Budgies are finicky, troublesome birds. If their needs are met, they will usually perform their little hearts out for you. However,

it may be that she hasn't consented to mate with the cock. In that case, she may do better with another mate. If there is poor physical contact between the Budgies' cloacas when they copulate, the sperm won't reach the egg, and again you'll have infertile eggs. Are the birds trying to mate on loose or swingy perches? Are there feathers obstructing the male's vent which should be clipped back? Is one of the birds overweight or lame? Any of these possibilities could prevent the male from mounting the female effectively. Of course, as the birds grow older, they will become less fertile and have to be retired from producing their own young, although they may make excellent foster parents if given fertile eggs from other nests.

If the eggs are fertile but the chicks die before they hatch, it it likely that the hen's diet didn't contain enough protein to give the eggs enough food to last through 18 or more days in the shell. Remember to have protein food that she likes available to her every day once breeding season begins. Sometimes chicks die because the humidity is so low that their shells become too hard to crack; however, it's unlikely, and you can do more harm than good by compulsively spraying eggs. If the humidity in the bird room is very low, you can use a humidifier to raise it to a more comfortable level.

Even more heartbreaking is when the babies hatch out successfully, but die a few days later just when their growth rate was about to spurt. Again, too little protein is the usual culprit. As you can see, a cheap diet is no bargain since it cheats you of chicks! It's also possible that a bacteria, mold, or other disease-producer killed the babies, since youngsters succumb to many ailments that adult Budgies are unaffected by. The nest box should be removed, cleaned and dried thoroughly between each brood. If mites have been a problem, the whole cage should be cleansed between broods and treated with one of the safe sprays available in pet stores. Food and water drinkers should always be spotless, but the one time you should never slack off is during breeding season since carelessly cleaned vessels can permit the growth of bacteria and other maladies.

There! It may seem like a lot of information thrown at you at once, but it really isn't so hard. Alertness and problem prevention are the keys to good breeding, and they are the keys to good health as well.

An adult male Budgie will have a bright blue colored cere (area above the beak) while a young male will have a pinkish to purple colored one.

COPING WITH INJURIES AND ILLNESSES

Contrary to what you may have heard, you don't have to give up on a sick Budgie. As more people are developing an interest in pet birds, more vets are studying their problems and diseases. More and more pet Budgies *can* be helped, even cured of such serious illnesses as ornithosis, the so-called "parrot fever." Your chances are better, of course, if you have located an avian vet before an emergency strikes. If you can't get a local recommendation from a bird-keeping friend or club, you can write to the Association of Avian Veterinarians, P.O. Box 299, East Northport, NY 11737, for the name of vets near you who are interested in helping birds. Although the vet trip may cost more than the Budgie, it's often useful to take a new bird in to the vet for a checkup so that the doctor can become familiar with your bird and advise you concerning any potential health problems. If you don't have the Budgie cleared by a vet, it's important to keep it away from any other birds you may own for a full 30 days to make sure it hasn't brought home anything contagious.

Once the Budgie is settled in, the key to avoiding future problems is prevention. Clipped wings, good grooming of beak and claws, and attention to the condition of its environment can prevent injury. An excellent diet and clean home, combined with frequent rests from breeding, help the Budgie resist disease. Boredom, poor diet, or filth encourage disease. Notice the psychological factor. A Budgie should have something to do and someone to do it with; its companion can be a mate with which it rears young, or an avian pal with which it explores the latest toys, or a human friend who teaches it tricks and games, but it must have a companion!

Still, even if we do everything perfectly, sickness and injury can strike, so you need to be aware of the possibility and alert to subtle changes in your Budgie's appearance and personality. A small bird has little room

This photo shows a budgie with a nasal granuloma (growth composed of granulation material) removed.

to store reserves, so it can exhaust itself quickly in the fight against disease. Fast action is often required to save its life. Yet, like most wild animals, Budgies have the infuriating habit of trying to conceal the fact that they don't feel well, a holdover from the wild where predators are quick to take advantage of sick or crippled animals. Often, the first sign that a Budgie is feeling ill is a sudden desire to withdraw from its normal activities. If a pet that's usually playful wants to nap all the time, you need to figure out what's wrong as soon as possible.

Check closely for signs of injury or disease, not that you should attempt to make a diagnosis on your own. Even a vet must often employ lab tests or specialized equipment to pin down the specific cause of a Budgie's problem. For instance, respiratory ailments from mild "colds" to ornithosis can all look much alike; it takes a lab test to determine what disease agent is present and how it should be combatted. As a general rule, you can treat what looks like a relatively mild problem at home by employing the use of isolation and warmth to let the Budgie's body fight the disease itself, while severe symptoms or problems that continue past a day or two call for a trip to the veterinarian's.

Isolation and warmth are best provided by a hospital cage. Nice models are available from advertisers in the bird-fancy magazines and some bird specialty shops, but you can make your own with a small travel cage and heating pad. The typical hospital cage is short, to force the bird to rest, but it's somewhat elongated so that you can put the source of 85 or 90°F heat on one side so that the Budgie can move away if it feels too warm. Often, however, it will be more than glad to recover near the heat in order to reserve its body's fuel supplies, particularly if it's eating poorly. (The normal body temperature of a bird is well over 100°F, so a Budgie with a slight fever can burn through an enormous amount of body fat in days or hours.) Food and water should be in easily accessible spots on the floor, with favorite treats among them to tempt weak appetites. Partially cover the cage to give privacy, a primal need with a sick bird, but leave an opening for fresh air. If you try to give one of the pet store remedies that are added to water, sweeten it with a little orange juice to make it more palatable, or the Budgie may stop drinking. And a time of sickness is no time for a Budgie to give up drinking! Again, if there is no improvement within a couple of days, see your vet for help.

COMMON BUDGIE PROBLEMS

You should be aware of the most common Budgie problems so that you can

Feather picking usually develops in a bird due to dry skin conditions or a dietary condition. However, after the cause has been found and remedied, the feather picking has become a habit that is very hard to break.

take action against them. It is a fact that many Budgies with unclipped wings are injured each year when they fly into walls or other surfaces at full speed. Untame birds are at highest risk, but even a normally calm pet can become startled and forget where it is. Concussion, broken wings, or broken legs are all treatable if you apply first aid for shock and get the bird to a vet as quickly

as possible. The best "shock treatment" is, of course, warmth combined with an enclosed space such as a travel cage to prevent the Budgie from thrashing around and injuring itself further. Cover the cage while it's in transit, for privacy and warmth. Another common injury occurs when ringed or long-nailed Budgies get a foot trapped in a loose hardware staple or other small trap. Quickly staunch blood with direct pressure, extricate the foot if you can, apply first aid for shock, and rush to the vet. Call the office for advice if you can't work the foot free. Try to stay calm. Your Budgie isn't doomed. These birds can live perfectly happy lives with only one foot, although they can no longer position for proper mating and thus cannot breed. A Budgie who has scalded itself by trying to land in boiling water or bathe under a hot tap should also be treated for shock and taken to the vet. A little burn ointment may help soothe it while in transit.

There are several common diseases that you should be on guard against. A particularly pesky one is "French Molt," in which young birds (usually about five to six weeks old) begin an excessive molt of tail and wing feathers. The cause isn't known, although it may be a virus. French Molt is also linked to receiving a low protein crop milk in the early

A particularly pesky disease is French Molt. It is when young birds (usually about five to six weeks old) begin an excessive molt of tail and wing feathers.

weeks of life, so perhaps the viral agent cannot get a foothold in the system if the parents are well fed. It also occurs more often in the offspring of a pair going to nest for the third time without a rest break, which we know exhausts the parents' nutrient reserves and may affect the quality of crop milk they can offer their babies. Good diet and rest periods are therefore the best preventions. Consult your vet for recommendations if the problem has already appeared. Sometimes French Molt clears up by itself after the next molt, but you can't count on it.

At the other end of the spectrum, we have the diseases of old age. The most common are similar to diseases found in older humans: tumors, diabetes, and gout. Since Budgies are extremely susceptible to tumors, you should make a habit of checking your pet for any suspicious lumps and bumps; most are benign and can often be removed. Diabetes, often accompanied by unusual thirst, can often be treated with insulin. Don't be squeamish about learning to inject your pet if that is what's called for; it can lead a happy, normal life with the disease under control. Gout due to kidney or liver dysfunction can cut off the blood supply to its feet, making perching uncomfortable or impossible; unfortunately, we don't know how to prevent or cure this disease, although vet treatment can ease the symptoms. You cannot catch any of these serious diseases from your bird, nor can you give tumors, diabetes, or gout to your pet.

All ages may be bothered by infections and parasites, although quarantining new birds away from any others for 30 days and providing excellent care will prevent many problems. Scaly mite, a microscopic parasite that encrusts the beak or leg with a white deposit, is very common in Budgies. It usually has to be transmitted by direct contact since it spends its whole life on the bird, so isolating the affected Budgies will prevent the disease from spreading. If treating the affected area with a small amount of mineral oil doesn't cure the problem, a prescription medication from the vet should finish the job. Red mites, which feed on birds at night and then leave to conceal themselves in the cracks of the cage and nest boxes during the day, can cause itching and discomfort in older birds while stealing so much blood from nestlings that the vulnerable babies die. If you suspect red mites, cover the cage with a

Many Budgies with unclipped wings are injured each year when they fly into walls or other surfaces at full speed.

white cover at night and shine a light on it later; if the mites are present, you'll see tiny red specks moving across the cloth as they leave your Budgies. To rid yourself of these pesky critters, you must clean all cracks and crevices of perches, nest boxes, swings, feeders, toys, and cages. A real pain! It's better to prevent an infestation in the first place by buying one of the many fine sprays or "bird protector" devices sold in pet stores.

A third common parasite, *Giardia*, makes its home in a Budgie's intestines, often causing poor digestion or large, discolored, smelly feces. After examining the wastes to diagnose the problem, the vet can prescribe a medication to kill the parasite.

Finally, we come to the respiratory diseases. You cannot hope to do much more on your own than try to make a rough determination of the severity of the problem. If the Budgie is a little sleepy and sneezy, putting it in the hospital cage for a day or two may be all you need. But if it has a nasal discharge, or its symptoms have persisted despite warmth and isolation, you must go to a vet who can make tests in order to prescribe the proper drug.

One possible respiratory infection is properly called Ornithosis, or Clamydiosis, although it is known to the public as Psittacosis, or "Parrot Fever." Any bird can carry it, not just parrots, so the name is unfair

and inaccurate. (Pigeons, both feral and domesticated, seem to be the number-one carriers of the disease.) A diagnosis of ornithosis is no longer a cause for panic, since the Budgie will usually recover quickly when treated with modern drugs. In the unlikely event that you contract the disease from your Budgie, today's medication will cure you as well. Of course, if you contract flu or pneumonia-like symptoms, you have to do your part and let your doctor know that you keep birds so that he or she can test for the possibility.

With care, quick thinking, and a little luck, your pet Budgie can be one of the growing number of feathered senior citizens.

Although disease and injury will always be with us, I hope you have been encouraged by our quick look at some of the advances in avian medical science. A sick bird doesn't have to be a dead bird, not if you keep a cool head and seek timely help. With care, quick thinking, and a little luck, your pet Budgie can be one of the growing number of feathered senior citizens.

RESOURCES

If your heart has been captured by the charming Budgerigar, you will undoubtedly want to learn more about these winning birds. There are two paths to gaining more information about Budgies: getting actively involved with other fanciers through a local bird club and gaining knowledge from breeders all over the world by studying some of the vast amounts of literature available on these beloved creatures. For most people, a mix of the two approaches is best; despite inclusion in an active club, most breeders and exhibitors continually scan the fancy press for new developments. For some people, however, an emphasis on one or the other resources may be more appropriate. An elderly fancier, for example, may get the most benefit from sharing information in a social setting, while a busy person with a more casual interest may glean all he or she needs to know from a monthly perusal of the popular cage-bird magazines.

Bird clubs, you'll find, are a great way to meet other fanciers with their own ideas and innovations for raising fine Budgies. Some expert breeders may seem secretive, but most are like experts in any other field, anxious to share their hard earned experience and knowledge. A sincere show of interest is often all you need to get an earful (or more) of valuable information.

If you're thinking about breeding for show, joining the national society and a nearby local organization are especially important since they'll keep you up-to-date on the show schedule and related matters. Getting to know your competition is useful as well as fun for many reasons, not least of which is that you'll get a chance to buy any high-quality birds put on sale before most outsiders even know they're available. And, of course, it's always nice to be able to see what other breeders are doing.

SHOWING YOUR BUDGIE

Before you leap into exhibiting your Budgies, you should visit a few shows and carefully examine the champion birds. Compare the winning Budgerigars with the "standard," the ideal specimen that breeders work toward. Then compare the best bird to the runners up. What qualities do all the winners share? Which quality distinguishes the "best in show" from a best in its division? Intelligence and steadiness are as important as perfect adherence to the standard, since a bird that cowers in a corner can hardly compare to a bird that sits proudly for the judge's admiration. Although most show Budgies are raised in too great a quantity to get the early personal attention they need to become pets, they must be tame enough to enjoy (or at least feign indifference to) the hustle and bustle of show time. Picked and trained to the show cage relatively late, they require patience and gentle handling on the part of the breeder. Are you up to the challenge?

Your intelligence is tested too, since you will need to acquire a basic knowledge of Budgie genetics in order to plan a breeding program. Don't groan. I doubt that anyone comprehends everything they are reading the first time they work through a chapter on genetic selection, but after some trial and error with actual birds you will start to understand. Seeing the results of your work makes the difference.

In sum, the beautiful Budgerigar will take you as far as you want to go. You can enjoy the antics of a semitame pair, train an individual to talk and play, breed a batch of beautiful youngsters, or go all the way to total immersion in a champion breeding project. The point is to enjoy! But then you can hardly help enjoying the beautiful, loving, playful Budgerigar.

INDEX

Page numbers in **boldface** refer to illustrations.